THE FUTURE IS FEMALE

ALTERNATOR BOOKS™

# Changemakers in MUSIC

## Women Leading the Way

NGERI NNACHI

Lerner Publications ◆ Minneapolis

*This book is dedicated to every woman with the sound of music within. May she find the support to share it with us all.*

Lerner Publications Company
An imprint of Lerner Publishing Group, Inc.
241 First Avenue North
Minneapolis, MN 55401 USA

For reading levels and more information, look up this title at www.lernerbooks.com.

Main body text set in Aptifer Sans LT Pro Medium.
Typeface provided by Linotype AG.

**Designer:** Athena Currier
**Lerner team:** Martha Kranes

**Library of Congress Cataloging-in-Publication Data**

Names: Nnachi, Ngeri, author.
Title: Changemakers in music : women leading the way / Ngeri Nnachi.
Description: Minneapolis : Lerner Publications, 2024. | Series: The future is female (alternator books®) ; 01 | Includes bibliographical references and index. | Audience: Ages 8–12 | Audience: Grades 4–6 | Summary: "Women have been groundbreakers in music of all genres. Young readers will discover changemakers from the past and present and their musical accomplishments. Then they are encouraged to make their own music"— Provided by publisher.
Identifiers: LCCN 2023014603 (print) | LCCN 2023014604 (ebook) | ISBN 9798765608852 (library binding) | ISBN 9798765624999 (paperback) | ISBN 9798765618349 (epub)
Subjects: LCSH: Women singers—Biography—Juvenile literature. | Women musicians—Biography—Juvenile literature. | BISAC: JUVENILE NONFICTION / Biography & Autobiography / Women
Classification: LCC ML82 .N56 2024  (print) | LCC ML82  (ebook) | DDC 782.42164092/52 [B]—dc23/eng/20230411

LC record available at https://lccn.loc.gov/2023014603
LC ebook record available at https://lccn.loc.gov/2023014604

Manufactured in the United States of America
1-1009547-51563-6/26/2023

# Table of Contents

# INTRODUCTION

## Award-winning Musician

**On May 4, 1959, Ella Fitzgerald won big at the first Grammy Awards.** She took home not one but two Grammys, becoming the first Black woman Grammy winner.

Fitzgerald kept making history. In 1967 she became the first Black woman to earn the Recording Academy Lifetime Achievement Award. Her songs and powerful voice changed music. She also opened doors for other women in music.

Fitzgerald sings in 1959.

From playing instruments to producing songs, women are involved in every part of creating music. Not every female musician can be covered in these pages. But the women in this book have changed music and how people enjoy it.

# CHAPTER 1

# Strong Singers

**Some women let their voices be heard through singing.** These musicians aren't afraid to belt out their tunes.

## A New Sound

Taylor Swift released her first album at the age of sixteen. It sold over five million copies. Taylor quickly became a country star and released three more albums. In 2014 Swift released her first full pop album. People loved her new sound, and she won a Grammy for Album of the Year.

Swift received the Woman of the Decade award in 2019.

In 2019 Swift became *Billboard*'s Woman of the Decade. She continues to put out music and win awards.

## Breaking Records

Robyn Rihanna Fenty, known as Rihanna, was born in Barbados. She brings the sounds of Barbados into her pop and rhythm-and-blues (R&B) songs. In 2005 Rihanna released her first single, and people around the world loved it. This gained her fans before her first album came out later that year. At twenty-three, she was the youngest person to have ten songs become number one on *Billboard*'s list.

Rihanna performs at the 2023 Super Bowl Halftime Show.

With eight albums, Rihanna has sold over 250 million records. She has also won awards for her music. She has nine Grammy Awards and twelve American Music Awards. She has broken six Guinness World Records in music. She broke the record for female artist with the most US number one singles in a year in 2010. She also reached one billion streams on YouTube with her song "Stay."

## Following Her Destiny

Beyoncé Knowles started her music career at nine years old. She was the lead singer of the R&B group Destiny's Child. Seven years later, the group signed a recording contract. They became famous and released several albums.

In 2003 Queen Bey released her first solo album *Dangerously in Love*. The album included the first songs she had written. Destiny's Child released another album before breaking up. Beyoncé continued to perform and release music

Beyoncé (*center*) sings as part of Destiny's Child in 2001.

Beyoncé performs on tour in 2023.

by herself. Fans were amazed by her powerful voice. As of early 2023, Beyoncé has been nominated for eighty-eight Grammy Awards and won thirty-two. She is the most awarded and nominated Grammy artist.

# CELEBRATING WOMEN

The *Billboard* Women in Music event celebrates women in the music industry. It started in 2007 as a small gathering and became an award show in 2015. The ceremony takes place once a year.

Singer SZA receives an award at the Billboard Women in Music event in 2023.

## Amazing Opera Singer

Marian Anderson was one of history's most celebrated singers. She sang a range of songs from opera to spiritual songs. In 1925 Anderson entered a singing contest and won. She sang with the New York Philharmonic after winning. She toured around the world performing for audiences.

Anderson singing at the Lincoln Memorial in 1955

In 1939 she wanted to perform a concert in Washington, DC. But the owners of the hall that was chosen didn't let her because she was Black. Many people stood with Anderson. Instead, she performed at the Lincoln Memorial. She sang in front of seventy-five thousand people. In 1955 Anderson became the first Black singer to perform with the Metropolitan Opera. Later, she earned a Grammy Award for Lifetime Achievement.

## Hall of Famer

Dolly Parton is known for combining pop and country. After high school, Parton moved to Nashville, Tennessee. Soon after, she joined singer Porter Wagoner on his television show. For seven years Parton sang country songs and gained fans. She put out thirteen albums with Wagoner.

Parton (*left*) sings with Wagoner in 1967.

Parton at the Rock & Roll Hall of Fame ceremony in 2022

Later, Parton left the show and was a solo artist. She wrote and recorded songs for her new album. The Country Music Association named her Female Vocalist of the Year two years in a row. Parton began to add a pop sound to her songs. Her music changed what people thought country and pop could be. She was inducted into the Country Music Hall of Fame in 1999 and the Rock & Roll Hall of Fame in 2022.

# CHAPTER 2

# Incredible Instrumentalists

**From strumming on a guitar to banging on a drum, instrumentalists play an important part in music.** Discover how these women steal the show.

## Recording Artist

At fourteen, Carol Kaye began her musical career playing jazz guitar. She played gigs with other musicians. Later, she played on several album recordings for famous artists. Kaye often played jazz bass. But when a bassist didn't show up for a recording, Kaye picked up the electric bass.

Kaye plays for a recording in the 1960s.

She recorded hits with hundreds of musicians. Kaye created her own sound playing with a hard pick. It brought out a strong bass sound during a time when there was a demand for a clicky sound with short notes. She played for television and movie scores. Kaye went on to write books on how to play the bass, and teach bass players.

# CREATING HER OWN RHYTHM

Cindy Blackman Santana is a soulful drummer. At three years old, she asked for her first set of drums. She's always loved hitting things to make rhythms.

In the 1980s, she became a street performer in New York City. Blackman then began recording her own records. She toured around the world with other musicians creating beats and exciting crowds. She also wrote and sang on the song "I Remember."

Blackman plays the drums in 2013.

> "[Music is] a way to share light with millions of people. They don't need to speak your language, have your beliefs, or be in the same place you are. The music speaks, it channels good energy, and makes a difference in people's lives."
>
> —CINDY BLACKMAN SANTANA

## Playing with Passion

Sarah Chang is a famous violinist. At five years old, she auditioned and was accepted at Juilliard, a competitive music school. Three years later, Sarah was a soloist for the New York

Chang plays in 2007.

# SUPER PERCUSSIONIST

Evelyn Glennie is the first solo percussionist to make it a full-time job. Being hard of hearing helped her grow closer to music.

Glennie performs in 2012.

> "My career and my life have been about listening in the deepest possible sense. Losing my hearing meant learning how to listen differently, to discover features of sound I hadn't realized existed. Losing my hearing made me a better listener."
>
> —EVELYN GLENNIE

Philharmonic. At eleven years old, she put out her first album. Soon she was performing over a hundred concerts each year.

Chang continued to put out new albums and earn awards. A magazine named her one of twenty powerful women taking charge. In 2011 she was named an official artistic ambassador by the US Department of State.

Chang (*right*) performs with an orchestra in 2012.

# CHAPTER 3

# Behind the Songs

**Some women make their mark on music in ways other than singing or playing an instrument.** They produce songs, conduct orchestras, write music, and more.

### Head of an orchestra

Marin Alsop is the first woman to be the head of a major orchestra in the US, South America, Austria, and Britain. She grew up playing piano and violin. After playing violin in an orchestra and a jazz group, Alsop studied conducting. A conductor directs an orchestra during a performance. Alsop became an associate conductor at Richmond Symphony in Virginia.

In 2002 she founded a program to help women conductors. Later, the program was renamed in her honor, the Taki Alsop Conducting Fellowship. In 2005 she was the first conductor to become a MacArthur fellow. This award is given to talented and creative people.

Alsop (*left*) conducts singer Jennifer Hudson and an orchestra in 2021.

# EXCITING ENGINEER

Angela Piva is an audio engineer and producer. Albums she worked on have sold millions of copies.

Music recording equipment

## Creative Composer

Gabriela Lena Frank is an award-winning composer. She was born with hearing loss and started playing the piano when she was four years old. Her piano teacher told her to try mixing styles. Gabriela started composing songs.

Frank plays her piece in 2003.

Frank went to college and studied music and composition. She brings her Peruvian, Chinese, Lithuanian, and Jewish backgrounds into her songs. In 2017 the *Washington Post* named her one of the thirty-five most important women composers in history. That year Frank opened the Gabriela Lena Frank Creative Academy of Music to help beginner composers. Frank has composed for many orchestras and symphonies.

## Super Songwriter

Ester Dean is a singer, producer, and songwriter. She was singing backstage at a music concert when a producer heard her. He set up a meeting with her and was amazed by her singing and songwriting. Dean signed a music deal and put out her first single.

She wrote hits for Rihanna including "Where Have You Been." Dean also wrote Katy Perry's "Firework" and Selena Gomez's "Come & Get It." She has also written songs for Beyoncé, Nicki Minaj, and others. She appeared on the TV show *Songland* where she judged songs that musicians wrote for famous artists.

Dean in a recording studio in 2015

TOKiMONSTA performs in 2019.

## Daring DJ

TOKiMONSTA is the stage name of Jennifer Lee. She started music as a pianist. In college, Lee joined open mic nights for DJs and producers. She created hip-hop, jazz, and electric sounds that people loved to dance to.

> "Be yourself and make music that speaks true to your heart."
>
> —TOKIMONSTA

She is a producer, songwriter, and DJ. She has put out many albums. In 2015 she had two brain surgeries and lost her ability to speak and hear. Lee healed from her surgeries and was later able to speak and hear again. She used her experience to create her third album. It earned a Grammy nomination for Best Dance/Electronic Album. She is the first Asian American and first woman to be nominated for the award.

TOKiMONSTA at a premiere in 2023

# CONCLUSION

## Making Your Music

**Women have made amazing contributions to music.** They sing our favorite songs. They compose powerful pieces. They amaze audiences by playing instruments. You can make your own contribution to music. If your school has music classes, you can sign up for them. You can write songs to express yourself. You can practice singing. You can make your own mark on the music world.

You can express yourself through music.

# Glossary

**album:** a recording of a set of songs

**composer:** a person who writes music

**conductor:** a person who stands in front of people while they sing or play musical instruments and directs their performance

**orchestra:** a group of musicians, led by a conductor, who play music together

**percussionist:** a person who plays musical instruments (such as drums, cymbals, or xylophones) by hitting or shaking them

**pick:** a small, thin piece of plastic or metal that is used to play a guitar or similar instrument

**producer:** a person who is in charge of a music recording

**score:** the music that is written for a movie or play

**solo:** when an artist performs or sings alone

# Source Notes

18    "About Cindy," Cindy Blackman Santana, accessed April 28, 2023, https://cindyblackmansantana.com/bio.

20    "Evelyn Glennie Biography," Evelyn Glennie, last updated January 24, 2023, https://www.evelyn.co.uk/about/biography/.

26    Ana Monroy Yglesias. "Meet the First-Time GRAMMY Nominee: TOKiMONSTA on Authenticity & Why 'Lune Rouge' Is "a Celebration of Life," Grammy, January 18, 2019,  https://www.grammy.com/news /meet-first-time-grammy-nominee-tokimonsta-authenticity-why -lune-rouge-celebration-life.

## Learn More

Britannica Kids: Marian Anderson
https://kids.britannica.com/kids/article/Anderson-Marian/352753

Britannica Kids: Taylor Swift
https://kids.britannica.com/students/article/Taylor-Swift/487625

Elizabeth, Jordannah. *She Raised Her Voice: 50 Black Women Who Sang Their Way into Music History*. Philadelphia: Running Press Kids, 2021.

Holleran, Leslie. *Dolly Parton: Diamond in a Rhinestone World*. Minneapolis: Lerner Publications, 2023.

Kawa, Katie. *Beyoncé: Making a Difference through Music*. New York: KidHaven, 2022.

Kiddle: Ester Dean Facts for Kids
https://kids.kiddle.co/Ester_Dean

Kiddle: Sarah Chang Facts for Kids
https://kids.kiddle.co/Sarah_Chang

Markovics, Joyce. *Ella Fitzgerald*. Ann Arbor, MI: Cherry Lake, 2023.

# Index

# Photo Acknowledgments

Image credits: Michael Ochs Archives/Getty Images, pp. 5, 13; Rich Fury/Getty Images, p. 7; Kevin Mazur/Getty Images, p. 8; Debra L Rothenberg/FilmMagic/Getty Images, p. 9; Kevin Mazur/Getty Images, p. 10; Christopher Polk/Billboard/Getty Images, p. 11; Bettmann/Getty Images, p. 12; Emma McIntyre/Getty Images, p. 14; GAB Archive/Redferns/Getty Images, p. 16; Antonio de Moraes Barros Filho/WireImage/Getty Images, p. 17; Dan Porges/Getty Images, p.18; Eileen Langsley/Popperfoto/Getty Images, p. 19; Lawrence K. Ho/Los Angeles Times/Getty Images, p. 20; Gotham/WireImage/Getty Images, p. 22; FilippoBacci/Getty Images, p. 23; Hiroyuki Ito/Getty Images, p. 24; Prince Williams/WireImage/Getty Images, p. 25; Timothy Norris/Getty Images, p. 26; Kayla Oaddams/WireImage/Getty Images, p. 27; Tim Platt/Getty Images, p. 29.

Cover: Tytus Zmijewski/EPA/Shutterstock (Cindy Blackman); AP Photo/zz/KGC-11/STAR MAX/IPx (Beyonce); AP Photo/zz/John Nacion/STAR MAX/IPx (Taylor Swift).

Design Elements: Old Man Stocker/Shutterstock, p. 1; MPFphotography/Shutterstock, p. 1; schab/Shutterstock, p. 1.